FABER NEW POETS

IN THE SAME SERIES

Joe Dunthorne

faber and faber

First published in 2010
by Faber and Faber Ltd
Bloomsbury House
74–77 Great Russell Street
London WC1B 3DA

Typeset by Faber & Faber Ltd
Printed in England by T. J. International Ltd, Padstow, Cornwall

ACKNOWLEDGEMENTS

Thanks to *The Edgeless Shape*, *Five Dials*, *Magma*,
Manhattan Review, *New Welsh Review*, *Penned in the Margins*,
Poetry Review, *Stop Sharpening Your Knives* and *Tears in the Fence*
who first published some of these poems and to *Newsnight Review*
and *The Verb* where they were first broadcast. Thanks to
Matthew Hollis, Maya Thirkell, Clare Pollard, Homework
and Todd Swift's Maida Vale workshop for their work
on these poems. Thanks also to my friends and family.

A CIP record for this book
is available from the British Library

ISBN 978-0-571-24999-2

2 4 6 8 10 9 7 5 3 1

Contents

Worship

When picking your spot, look for a balance
of elements. Always show respect to those
wearing lower factors than you. Always check
downwind before shaking out your towel.

Lie back. Let the sand make a duplicate
of your spine. Match your breath to the tide.
Clear away all thoughts (now that wasn't
so tough). Let your body do the thinking.

On the backs of your eyelids, you will likely
see your childhood sweetheart in flames,
dowsed in lamp oil. This is natural.
Let her dance. You deepen by the hour.

Cave Dive

Every sixteen metres of depth is equivalent to
one alcoholic drink.
– MAURO BERTOLINI, *The Diver's Handbook*

He remembers being six,
lying on his back beneath a kitchen chair,
gazing up at his father's unmapped nostrils,
his mother's skirt riffling past like a spotted
eagle ray. Underneath the dining table,
he found pencil marks: a quarter-circle
and two words underscored. *Possible Extension.*
Back then, it was a code or perhaps
the solution to a code.
                              On the cave bed,
it takes a blue whale's long blink to fathom
what one plus one turns into. The sky peers
down from blue-green slots like the lamp fittings
of his youth. His slow mind thinks time
is just another surface, he can pass through
the swirling halocline that keeps us
from our pasts:
                    the fresh and the preserved.
Back in his father's study, pouring a bag
of marbles across the rug. In the glow
from the tentacled lampshade, he holds
up his Bosser, sees himself swimming
in its spiral reef.
                        Letting drift his aqualung,
he is either young or drunk. From his lips
he scatters balls of glass.

Eating Out

Dumpsters simply brimming
with send backs and leftovers, black sacks
full of nummy slop: coconut pannacotta,
truffle honey mozzarella, California bouillabaisse
and even if you mush the food together
I'll bet it still tastes pretty good
but then, what of the down-by-luck
table-salt types: smelling like asparagus piss,
little half-healed cuts on their nose bridges,
you'd think they'd be allowed to lick a strand
of marinated pig fat from inside a bin bag
but no, because even the tossed-out
slops still represent the chef
and they say a restaurant's reputation
is only equal to its clientele so the good places
have a cage, a big steel cage
in the alley out the back to protect
the scraps from these poor sods
with their bellies cramping
and their sunburnt eyelids
and I mean it makes you feel
terribly helpless
really, forty slightly
overdone scallops going to rot
in a cage, imagine.

The Actual Queen

Ma'am, I am imagining
you at your worst:
watching a wet-lipped
girl type-set your cutlery.
You're hating her neediness.
You think the girl is certainly
attractive, if not exactly
beautiful and you imagine
an alternative life for her
where she is a waitress
in a chequerboard pie shop,
pickled onions in a clamp jar,
glowing like pearls. A dozen
older men desire her. Her apron
the item they imagine removing.
There is just one gent for whom
she doles out extra liquor.
In the back room, watched
by crates of royal russet apples,
they struggle to articulate
the simple, awkward
love that could only grow
in a given structure, say
that of the waitress to the waited.

Filters

My big sister rings to say she is riding around
on the back of Richard's motorbike
and would I like to meet for a drink
Richard is a married man.
My sister is gay and I am always
dropping this into conversation.

She has a helmet under her arm
and a rum with ginger beer.
I sometimes ask my sister
if she has dismantled the patriarchal hegemony yet,
which is a joke. Her ex-girlfriend says
that every bar should have non-male space,
just like you have non-smoking.

We're talking about marathon training.
The pub is beneath a brick railway bridge. The light
is greenish and you can feel the invisible trains.
Out front, they're selling oysters on a school desk.
My sister says, How about it?
When we were young, we used to fight.
She chipped my tooth with a door stop.
I will eat anything.

The oysters smell of tin foil.
They are still alive.

My sister thinks I should chew a few times;
Richard says I should swallow it whole.
The creature is in my mouth
and now I must decide.

Sestina for My Friends

I know what my friends think
because of the things they say:
'Joe, you are shiny and worthwhile and always
thinking of others.' I am not so great.
I could name at least five people who are better,
overall. Here's one of my faults: I'm forever calculating

how to present myself in any given situation. Calculating
people give W. G. Sebald's *Rings of Saturn* as a gift, and think
that the person receiving the book will think better
of them. After reading it they will say:
'Joe – it was beautiful, I mean, he's like the great
gramps I never had. He even made Suffolk compelling.' I always

give *Rings of Saturn* as a gift, sometimes even to boys. *Always*
is too much. I have given it twice, if I'm calculating
honestly. Once to a girl who thought I was great
for just over a month until she suspected, correctly, that I think
I am more interesting than her. If I say
that the boy I gave it to was far better

at football than me, then I think you understand. Better
to be left for dead on the right wing, always
knowing that the boy who embarrassed you – let's say
his name's Luke – has this book in his bedroom. I'm calculating
that he won't have sold it because he thinks,
nay hopes that one day he might read it, this great

and clever book that was a gift from a friend who's not great
at football but by God, he's got a brain and, ultimately, it's better
to have enormous thoughts than to be almost semi-pro. I think
great people don't have these sorts of thoughts. I always
keep my mauled copy somewhere half-inconspicuous, calculating
the spot where guests will see it, sure, but they will not say

I bet Joe put that there so I see it. More likely, they'll say,
huh, such a clever book just lying there next to his football boots.
   It's great
to know someone like Joe who's clever but doesn't rub your face
   in it. Calculating
people are some of the worst in existence. This poem is better
for its honesty. Even when I admit this stuff, my friends can always
fall back on my honesty. He thinks

too much, they think. We'd best not say
anything about that sestina. He'll always be great
to us, better than great, more like excellent. Or this is what
   I'm calculating.

Deaths I'll Never Live Through #3

Yucatan, Mexico, 1009

Beheaded on top of Coba,
relieved of my freight like a cab
unhitched from its trailer, down
a hundred and sixty epiphanies,
one for each step: *at last*, I get you,
Jackson Pollock, now I'm spraying red
in cartwheels, past rows of painted
sports fans who wouldn't know
a masterpiece if it attacked them
with an axe, who wouldn't know
conquistadores if they turned up
in massive boats, and bouncing by
I try to say: laugh now, 'cause
soon your temple's only human
sacrifice will be the lopping off
of loved ones' heads in cruelly
angled photographs – but no one
likes a smartarse from the future,
so they slow clap as I pinball
to a meeting with my pals, previous
contestants, stacked like profiteroles,
watching from the gravel pit:
the heads of bad sports, bad poets,
the heads of the purest children,
all smiling up, *I am coming
my sweets, I have so much news.*

A Disastrous Campaign in Bohemia

In a gutted outside broadcast van
we took off for the Altamont Speedway,
throwing ashtrays to the wind
– *set 'em free, Maria, set 'em free* –
and rode unwelcomed into Livermore,
took off our shirts, played hacky sack
on their fundamental lawns,
got sunburnt and called it napalm,
said we were sisters and brothers.

I made love to Maria in the Berkeley
fountain, let our bodies send
a message, let our mouths tend our bodies.
When the summer was over
and Charlie Manson's arrest reminded
us to call our families, the hopes
we'd hosted began to fade.
The college friends that we heard were dead
seemed even cooler now.

Future Dating

Sat along rotating laminate benches,
we wear scrolling badges that display:
Name – Favourite thing – Emotional state.
I am Joe – Money – Anxious
as Porcia – Old buildings – Extraordinary
swivels into view with art deco
cheekbones, sky-rise posture.
She speaks in intricate structures
with witty stucco asides
and is either marriage material
or a one-off demolition-fuck
in a room full of Lego.
I give her green as she dioramas
into Karen – Knitting – Distracted:
her chopsticks clicking
as though making a scarf
from her udon noodles,
our three minutes pass in excruciating
knit one purl one chit-chat.
She sucks up her tongue,
draws a frowning emoticon
in the air before swishing away
as Sylvia – Firearms – Impatient
appears: shotgun eyes, fingers twitching,
a bruise on her right shoulder
the colour of rock dust, she asks
for my favourite assassination
then lets off rounds
of semiautomatic laughter
while I press red and red
as Kate – Imperfections – Unclear
pulls up with semi-translucent hair.

I compliment her body, her lips,
the infinite detail of her eyes
but she says she can take no credit.
Then she's screaming, quietly,
that her battery's about to die
as she starts to fizz like an unearthed plug.

Afternoon Meditation at the Ecovillage

The focaliser's eyes pace back and forth
behind their lids. He inhabits his mind.
My stairwell's blocked with half-unpacked boxes.
One is labelled *my version of events* and rattles
when I shake it. I hear his throat creak
as the fifth dimension swings open.

What's he doing up there? How long
since he took the batteries out of the wall clock?
There's a knock at the tangible door.
Pottery's got the room from six. *You can't just
exit the attic dimensions, there are procedures, visas . . .*
Our diesel *Om* evokes a refuse freighter

pushing clear of the dock and – *like that* –
I'm among the gulls following its heap of landfill.
I realise I am *inside* myself, circling my innards.
One of the gulls says: 'Joe, our time is up.'
How true. My mind is alternately half-empty,
half-full at the sheer waste/dinner of it all.

Fill the Blanks

I meet all my girlfriends in the cereal aisle.
They cannot reach the _____.
We agree that it's the delicious flavour
of _____ that starts the day buzzing
like a swarm of _____. 'You are sweet,'
they say, 'and fibrous.' They see the child's seat
of my trolley is empty, which is my cue
to kiss them against the point of sale display.
'I'm _____,' I say, 'but you can call me ___.'
Their eyes are like bowls of _____
with too much milk, and I tell them as much.

They are in my bed. I have all the film tie-in toys
lined up on the mantelpiece. I have full-fat,
semi-skimmed, skimmed, but they just roll over
and keep sleeping. Their name is Phillipa,
please wake up.

All My Friends Regardless

All my friends regardless,
come to my garden and pretend to get along.
Please let me introduce the scientists. Yes,
he studies the behaviour of bees.
Friends from my childhood,
I do not think you stupid and boring.
Assistant editors, step away from the pond.
This man has written a dystopian
sci-fi novel; this man is an eco-carpenter.

I am on the roof, feeling so various,
astonished by my own width,
with water bombs in each hand.

Intelligent Animals

The pigs are happy
and we cannot understand why.
We mention heavy industry
but they shrug and make a contented sound
from deep inside their rectangular bodies.
What about the press, we say,
where a white man is worth fifty yellow ones?
They nuzzle the dirt and do a roly-poly.

We show them buckets of antiseptic.
We show them photos of cows on fire.
We show them a documentary
about intensive pig farming.

Alchemy

A freediver misjudging his weightbelt
is an aspirin exhaling in a tall glass
is sunlight burning through mist
is a medallion under a muscle vest.

Workshop Dream

All poets lived in one low-rise resort.
Sleepwalking, I climbed across the white
balconies to Sean O'Brien's apartment.
I expected him to be angry but he wasn't.
He said I was not the first poet to arrive
this way. Inside, Koch was cooking breakfast,
a Faber editor was applying after-sun
and there was a woman I'd not read.

We walked through the quadrant
in O'Brien's slipstream, noticing
everything worth noticing: the blanched
undersides of leaves, Szirtes's towel,
the memory of wet feet on stone.

We stepped on to the beach. The water
made the sound: cliché, cliché, cliché.
We shooed away the avant-garde,
who sold necklaces made from shattered
windscreen glass. *Tiny grains of sand*,
I added. Sean, our windbreak, shook his head
and pointed out to sea but there was nothing.
He advised us to look again and this time,
sure enough, on the surface in the troughs
between waves: a huge flock of addenda.